W9-COO-789

For Claudio, my rock
—J. Marzollo

To my rockin' *friends:*
Katy, Chris, and Zach
—J. Moffatt

The editors would like to thank Margaret Carruthers
of the American Museum of Natural History,
New York, for her expertise.

Cut-paper photography by Paul Dyer.

Photographs of rock samples on pages 30-31 as follows: Chalk and flint
samples, Breck P. Kent, photographer. Iron sample courtesy of B. Walsh,
J. Beckett, and M. Carruthers. All other rock samples supplied by Photo
Researchers — photographers: granite, Andrew J. Martinez; salt, François
Gohier; gold, Dan Suzio; sandstone, Joyce Photograghics; slate, Aaron Haupt;
diamond, Charles D. Winters; talc, Ben Johnson/Science Photo Library; coal,
Geoff Lane/CSIRO/Science Photo Library; petrified wood, Jim Steinberg.

No part of this publication may be reproduced in whole or in part, or stored in a
retrieval system, or transmitted in any form or by any means, electronic, mechanical,
photocopying, recording, or otherwise, without written permission of the publisher.
For information regarding permission,
write to Scholastic Inc., 557 Broadway, New York, NY 10012.

Text copyright © 1998 by Jean Marzollo.
Illustrations copyright © 1998 by Judith Moffatt.
All rights reserved. Published by Scholastic Inc.
Printed in the U.S.A.

ISBN 0-439-45167-1

SCHOLASTIC, HELLO READER!, CARTWHEEL BOOKS, and associated logos and
designs are trademarks and/or registered trademarks of Scholastic Inc.

16 15 14 13 12   40   10 11 12 13 14/0

I Am a Rock

by Jean Marzollo
Illustrated by Judith Moffatt

Cartwheel
·B·O·O·K·S· ®

SCHOLASTIC INC.
New York   Toronto   London   Auckland   Sydney
Mexico City   New Delhi   Hong Kong   Buenos Aires

Welcome to the
Rock Hall of Fame.
My name is Marble.
Come and meet
my friends.
Can you tell
who they are?

I am a famous granite rock. The Pilgrims stepped on me when they came to America. Who am I?

Plymouth Rock

I am white and tasty.
You can sprinkle me
on your food.
Who am I?

Salt

I am used for money
and jewelry.
Who am I?

Gold

I am melted
to make glass.
Glassblowers make
shapes from me.
Who am I?

Sandstone

You can write with me.
You can draw with me.
Who am I?

Chalk

I am flat enough to walk on.
I am flat enough to write on.
Who am I?

Slate

I dazzle! I sparkle!
I am a jewel!
I am also very hard.
People use me to cut glass.
Who am I?

Diamond

I am ground into powder.
People can shake me on
babies to keep them dry.
Who am I?

Talc

I hold heat well. People use me to make frying pans and wood-burning stoves. If I get wet, I rust. Who am I?

Iron

Strike me against a rock.
See the spark?
Campers can use me
to start fires.
Who am I?

Flint

I burn slowly.
People can use me
for heat and power.
Who am I?

Coal